THE SLATE SEA

Edited by
Paul Henry and Zed Nelson

THE CAMDEN TRUST

Foreword

A new bridge in the Lledr Valley, three short films, poetry readings and workshops, a photography exhibition at the Mostyn Gallery and this book, *The Slate Sea*. You can say all this began with my mother's death at 95, the last of her generation in our family. It dawned on me at the time that it wasn't just a mother we'd lost but most of our family's history, especially its anecdotal history.

Even when she was 95, questions she could answer were put off for another day. Who was dad's "best man" in their wedding photo which took pride of place on the sideboard? What was the recipe for the ravioli she made for Thanksgiving dinner? How did grandma and grandpa, illiterate farm workers from the south of Italy, manage to get to Chicago and then raise five children on grandpa's "business" of sharpening knives and repairing umbrellas from a cart he pushed around the streets of Chicago? Was it really true that great grandpa Ambrosia removed the central heating from his house because he said it ruined the wine he made in the basement? And what good deeds did uncle Guido do so that he was always referred to as uncle Deed? Then my mother died and answers to unasked questions died with her.

For nearly 25 years I've had a cottage, 'Aber', at Roman Bridge in the Lledr Valley, near the village of Dolwyddelan in North Wales. It's where my mother always came when visiting from Chicago. "Venice is pretty," she would say, looking out over the valley, "but Wales is beautiful." Her death, and all those unasked questions, inspired me to record the remembered past of my neighbours and everyday life in this sheep farming community.

But my personal curiosity soon grew to having "outsiders" – poets, a photographer, film makers – record, in their own ways, what they saw, heard and felt there. And then this too expanded, from "my" valley and village to two other communities found in this part of North Wales which were centred on slate and the sea: Blaenau Ffestiniog, which once "roofed the world" with its slate tiles, and Cwmorthin, the deserted slate village hidden above the town. The sea side of my project inhales the holiday air of Rhyl and Llandudno, popular resorts where thousands of factory and mine workers from the Midlands enjoyed a week or two's knees up – respite from their toil.

Twice, for a week each time, poets, a photographer, filmmakers, even two bridge designers, stayed at 'Aber'. I introduced them to my neighbours and the valley. They roamed the streets of Blaenau and the secretive ruins of Cwmorthin; also the chalk and cheese seaside towns of Rhyl and Llandudno. Their brief? "Write whatever you want about what you see, hear and feel in these places. Record in poetry and photos the past for the present generation and the present for future generations."

Some of the fruits of their labour are in this book. A wider selection, including films, was presented for an exhibition at the Mostyn Gallery. And the project goes on … In production is a musical film of Rhyl in the 50's and 60's, an era before holiday makers traded the sometimes Sunny Rhyl for package holidays to the almost always Sunny Med.

As well as offering a unique view of North Wales, it's my hope that this project will inspire similar ones and, on a more personal level, encourage readers to record their own family history. Ask questions before those with the answers are gone. The past is too precious to lose. It is the soil of our roots.

BOB BORZELLO

Introduction

For well over a century, the Conwy Valley Line has connected the three industries of slate quarrying, hill farming and seaside tourism. It has ferried the loves, griefs, laughter and stories of the people who survived by these means. Travelling the more intuitive lines of poetry and photography, this book offers a collection of responses to localities which have played host to these three, distinct aspects of Welsh life.

All of the work in *The Slate Sea* was commissioned by Bob Borzello, director of the Camden Trust, to whose Lledr Valley cottage two groups of poets, along with photographer Zed Nelson, journeyed for a week's residency in 2004 and 2014. Perhaps "visit", rather than "residency", more accurately describes the unusual time-span offered for creative response – brief enough to elicit spontaneous, lyrical reactions to new surroundings yet long enough to arouse curiosity about the history and people of the areas. Commissioned poems are generally written with a half-glance over one's shoulder. The very act of writing them feels … less private. The ensuing tension can either elevate or diminish the poet's art. I hope readers agree that the former has prevailed here.

With the exception of Bethesda-based Alys Conran, the commissioned poets hailed from mid, west and south Wales. Strangers in their own land, they neither *resided* nor passed through. They haunted, visiting farms, quarries, churches, piers … They talked to local luminaries, researched the stories that moved them. They read the landscape, its hills and waves, its "book of slate" – an image which is repeated in 'The Slate Sea'.

As the only poet who attended both the 2004 and 2014 visits, I was invited to collect what has largely emerged as a book of ghost poems, where people (dead or alive) and places are imbued with a sense of absence. A similar, haunting absence resonates through the photographs of Zed Nelson, none of which was taken in conscious response to the poems.

Some of the verse in these pages appears in the mother tongue of a country where the industrial and cultural heritage is as diverse as its landscape and coastline. *The Slate Sea* is testament to this diversity.

PAUL HENRY

I

THE VALLEY AND THE VILLAGE

History

Don't try to learn this place
in the pages of a history
but go up instead
to the disused quarry

where the water lies still
and black as oil
and the only chiselling
is that of the blackbird's song

drilling its notes
into the hillside's soil.

And there, beside the falls of moss,
pick yourself a blade of slate,
long as your arm, rusted,
metallic in sound.

Tap it with your heel,
then with your fingertips
at its leaves, gently
prise it apart.

And see how it becomes
a book of slate

in which you can read
a story of stone –
one that's written
throughout this valley

in every head, across every heart
and down the marrow of every bone.

OWEN SHEERS

Valley Vignettes

Inside the collie's twitching ear
a tractor is changing gear.

*

Rubbing two notes together
sparks a flame inside the heather.

*

All we had and all we are –
a dandelion seed in air.

*

Or running water: tick of stone
on stone, on stone, on stone …

*

The tortured nests are empty now,
the wind's instruments on boughs.

*

Inside the chained collie's eye
a field's shaken snowflakes fly.

PAUL HENRY

Pont Cwm Lledr

Bwa o bren sy'n eco
Uwchben y llif o'r llifio;
Gwnaed â llaw ganllaw gain
A fo ben bid bont i'n harwain.

Fe groeswn bontydd bywyd,
cymodi, a'u codi o'r newydd.
Er cerrig rhyd yn eu hyd islaw,
Ein troedle'n ynys heb frys, heb fraw.

MENNA ELFYN

Lledr Valley Bridge

Sighing inside the timber's bow
his saw's refrain, across the flow.
His hands are in this grain
and so hold yours again

as you cross to the other side.
Hold onto him now, your guide.
The river's rocks cannot hurt
the steady steps of your heart.

tr. CHRISTOPHER MEREDITH
and
PAUL HENRY

First Light

WILLIAM
Eldest son of Thomas and Mary Rostran (late of Crew,
Superintendent of the steam engines machinery on the line
and tunnel at Dolwyddelen) who departed this life by
falling under the wheels of the traction engine, June 12th 1877
AGED 13 YEARS AND 4 MONTHS

[In the graveyard of St Gwyddelan's church, Dolwyddelan]

And after all the stone taken,
tapped, drilled and blasted
from the mountain's side,
this – perhaps to pay.

A grave too short by at least a foot,
a mound of soil and shale beside
like the half-turned pages
of a half-read book,

and inside the coffin, his son,
his Abraham's sacrifice
to the job so many
say can't be done.

But as the last hymn fades
and the congregation peels,
already he can feel it
pulling him again.

The need for the tunnel's slow work
to begin once more,
so that when the last of the stone
finally gives,

he might be there,
as through a chink no larger than an eye
the first light enters in,
to penetrate the darkness, their doubt

and even, he hopes,
the heaviness of this book
already closing on his son
behind him.

OWEN SHEERS

Eglwys Dolwyddelan

Dolwyddelan Church

'O un annwyl yn huno- yn y bedd
Johnny bach sy yno
Hen gyfiawn rhown i'w gofio
Lech o aur ar ei lwch o'.
Corrisyn Roberts

Byw angau a wnawn yma
Yn y llan, a'r llanciau
Dan eu sang.

Camwn dros eu camre
Uwch noethlwm fyd diesgid
Heb esgus.

Baglu ar englyn- a'r enw
Yn gynnil
er afradlon yw bro ing.

Nid llachar, na llech aur
Ond llwydni
Cen ar gerfluniau

Oes arch bellach dan dywarchen?
Diddadl a dieiriau
Yw gweflau'r sych ddanadl.

Rho tro ar wae a wnawn yma:
Bachwyd y rhai bychain
I droell dyn a'i drallod.

Dau beth sy'n oeri'r byw-
Bedd llwm, ywen yn ddail-drwch-
un yn mynnu'r lle
a'r llall yn mynnu'r llwch.

MENNA ELFYN

Penamnen

I Bill a Mary yn Nolwyddelan, am lafur
cariad wrth adfer cartref Angharad James.

Dau greyr tal, ar ffrwst, yn codi pig,
A darfu arnom ar ein taith hyd lôn
Sarn Helen dawel, lle roedd Mai ar frig
A dau'n llafurio yno, mor ddi-sôn.
Ymysg y cloddio brwd, ai'r maen o'r garn
Yn groeso aelwyd drosom wrth i'w fflam
Ail fyw y gogoneddau, ddarn wrth ddarn
O ddrws y tŷ, i 'Glwt y Ddawns' a'i cham.
A throelli wnaethom ninnau yn y swae
Y sgidiau bach mewn simnai, mela'r mur,
A sigl sgwrs y pâr yn trin a gwau
Yr oes a fu, nes adfer dôl i'w thir.
Os cododd adar, yn y bore'n fras
Daeth dau i gadw nyth mewn cwmwd glas.

MENNA ELFYN

Penamnen

for Bill & Mary, who excavated the
Dolwyddelan house of Angharad James.

May is in every branch.
Two herons pass over us in the lane.
Sarn Helen is still. Spade on stone
will do for talk. Inch by inch,
year on year, we piece back the house
where Angharad James danced.

When the hearth stone's in place
and our jig-saw made
we'll dance, as she demanded, wild.
Inside the chimney, her ballet shoes
wait, small as a child's,
keep the company of bees.

While we work on, patient as stone,
beating our metal wings in the lane.

tr. PAUL HENRY
and MENNA ELFYN

Note. Angharad James (1677–1749), Dolwyddelan farmer, poet and harpist, used to make her workers dance as she played the harp.

Two Customers

I know a man who wears his life
like a loose summer jacket,
an inch wider at each shoulder,
a mile longer at the cuffs.
His beard grazes broad lapels
unshorn, unafraid of strangers.
Fluid about him when he laughs
the lining of his soul spills
and shines, in praise of empty pockets.

And I know a man who wears his life
like a too tight Sunday suit,
its waistcoat nailed to his chest
seven times. If I were his wife
I'd ask him to loosen the tie.
He keeps his money neatly pressed
against his heart, like the flower he gave,
once, to a girl, who closed its eye
inside a bible and kept it from the light.

PAUL HENRY

H. Ogwen
Evans
Teiliwr / Tailor
01492-650347

How to Kill

A fox can go through twenty in a night,
love bites so lethal to the neck and the head,
that even if they survive it's already too late
and three weeks later they still drop,
as if bitten again by some ghost fox.

But don't get me wrong, I'd never shoot the last of them.

The badger has two ways:
a couple of puncture wounds to the back of the head
and the liver sniffed out with a surgeon's skill,
or more often, skinned – the whole lamb
rolled from its body like a glove off a hand.

But still, I wouldn't shoot the last one.

The crows though, in hangman's hoods,
now there's a different story.
Dropping from the sky to stab out an eye
or to pick at their unripe tongues,
or worst of all, to open one up with its beak
and then leave it, panting through the last of its lungs.

Well, I'd kill them all if I could.
Every last one.

OWEN SHEERS

Liable to Floods

'Liable to floods' the farmer warned them.
And on the map, the letters arcing down the valley
in black and white
but still the major wouldn't listen –

tipping back his cap with one finger
and laying a fatherly hand on the farmer's shoulder
'Don't you worry Jack' he said,
'We've got this one covered.'

And so they made their camp,
a thousand tents across the valley floor,
but even then as the GI's tapped the steel
they felt the backbone of the rock, shallow beneath the soil.

For the next two days they trained
under Moel Siabod's shoulder.
Greenhorns from Kansas, Ohio and Iowa,
sweeping in a line

through the ditches, streams and bracken,
preparing for the landings on Utah and Omaha
pegged as yet to an unknown date
hung somewhere just over the horizon.

On the third night they slept to the sound
of the rain's fusillade and the artillery of thunder,
while outside, under cover of darkness
the river pulled herself up and spread her wings,

bleeding through the camp like ink from a broken cartridge.
The guards were woken by their tin cans and cups
set afloat and clinking against each other
like ghosts in celebration.

They raised the alarm but it was already too late
and the river, arming herself with their rifles,
flushing out the latrines, swallowing the jeeps,
gathered them all and ushered them off.

And as their camp beds became rafts,
gently lifted and spun, more than one GI
woke from dreams of home to sense,
just for a second, somewhere deep in the bone,

how suitable this was,
as if the weather had finally caught up with their lives –
this being taken at night without any say,
this being borne, this being swept away.

OWEN SHEERS

II

THE BURIED HEART

Catching the Light

'Breichled o dref ar asgwrn y graig' – Gwyn Thomas, *Blaenau*

A dam was built to catch it, as in a cupped palm
and when light was finally shed through the cracks
of the lake's slate fingers onto the bracelet-terraced
town, the wet windows fizzed under their grey brows,
and the muscling river of men was lit, and is lit again,
as they sway to their candle-dark labour in the black
bellied hill, clipping their tick-tock drip-along boots
left and right, and left up the hill's stair, cigarettes
ash down to the end from such an age of smoke, and
their rain turned up so hallelujah bright I catch it for
my wireless love, my network streets, my fuck it
news news news, my god! And birdsong on demand, oh
plug it in quick, this USB port sadness streaming rain, and
oh this rain of theirs charged up so whole I catch it.

ALYS CONRAN

Silicosis

Underground, in a clearing of throat, berthed
in a dug out bog pit, breathe. Lungs take in gaps
of air take cell breaths under, take stale vent
breath, buried sod cough and clod breath
and poor sod stuck in bed breath.

In a bad bed,
a clay-cold catarrh pit, in wheeze and spit, heave,
hit the roof, grieve, kick the slate quarry grit
and breathe. Oh breathe.

For wallowed breeze
on heather heath, for peat bog, fog bloom and
waning bracken's brown curl leaf, for upturned
earth half-lit by a going-down sun, and one breath
after one, like running things run.

For wide lungs
full of open sky, and a breath so full of heaven
this buried heart lifts between its beating wings.

ALYS CONRAN

The Slate Sea

Spirit of the quarry
we are not here for long.
You are lighter than air
and I loved your eyes
from the first stone's song,
spirit of the slate sea.

Deep in my coral quarry
the dusty bubbles rise
from miners and mariners,
the shoals of drowned choirs.
So many unsung songs
deep in the scaly quarry.

Is it not the same country,
the slate turning its tide
at the edge of the road,
a scree of waves toppling
over Crustacean Terrace?
Is it not the same place?

This tunnel leads to the sea.
Dig deeper, deeper…
and hold this spirit kiss
to help you breathe, my dear
between light and darkness.
This tunnel leads to the sea.

Spirit of the quarry
we are not here for long.
You are lighter than air
and I loved your eyes
from the first stone's song,
spirit of the slate sea.

PAUL HENRY

DU05
GXW

Nettles, Cwmorthin

Outside the ruin of Tŷ Manijar
they lean tall as men
sedate and dusted in brief sunlight
singing a noiseless air
to the broken houses,
to the high lake:

We stand where once you cracked your sinews
spring bad flowers
where your boots scraped rock

and oh, the heaviness of all your effort
whispers only in the slide of rubble
in capless walls packed Aztec tight,
unpeopled

and yes, this song's an irony
a kind of laughing,
each chorus in its season coming back
and always strong and light
and taunting.

With no more effort than it takes to be
ourselves
we make each year our feather shape in air,
us subtle flowers armoured in ground glass,
singing in the wake of all your striving,
choking the stone gates where
your children passed.

CHRISTOPHER MEREDITH

Dail poethion, Cwmorthin

Ger murddun tŷ'r rheolwr
fe safant yn gôr
dan gorongylchoedd euraidd
heulwen hafau byr

a chanu maent
yn ddi-sain, heb arweinydd,
i'r cartrefi chwâl,
at wyneb dedwydd y llyn uchel:

Ymgrymwn yn ein cân
lle cynt bu rhwygo gewyn,
ein hadau yn alawon
lle'r aeth eich hoelion trwm
yn groch ar graig

a gwatwar yw ein hemyn
ein gwên yn weiren bigog,
pob cytgan yn ei dymor
yn dychwelyd
yn ysgafndroed, yn gryf,
yn chwerthin

ac mae trymder eich ymdrechion yn ddim
ond sibrwd rwbel yn y nos
dim ond mudandod y gwefusau tyn
ym meini nadd y muriau
heb do, heb drigolion

a phob blwyddyn codwn floedd
ein buddugoliaeth, ein bodoli,
ninnau'r blodau cyfrwys,
gan dagu'r pyrth o grawiau
lle'r aethoch chi.

Blue Blood

What kept Sion from forgetting what it was
his father used to say about his veins
was the flag that waved the name *Koblenz*
enamelled to the castle on the spoon
with which he'd tap the teacup
once the tale was told, as if to send
the memory to bed; of how he'd flown
spitfires until the Germans had shot down
his plane with poisoned darts the shade
of ink that had seeped into his blood.
Except they hadn't. Nor had his dad

unhooked a cockpit door nor heard the engine
sing inside his bowels as the undercarriage
left the ground. His dad's heroism was
the unspoken kind, where you balance
on ladders for forty years down a mine
from which you long to escape, perhaps by
flying high, whilst all the time climbing
lower to reach the veins of slate that led
towards the centre of the earth, purpling
the air before turning his own blood
blue with the silicosis that whispered this.

SAMANTHA WYNNE-RHYDDERCH

Portrait

They say it scraped the apex of the bridge
on all three rehearsals to evacuate
the National Gallery to a hollow mountain
north of Blaenau, but on that September day
in 1941 *Charles I on Horseback* rode by
in a canted transit case with
three-quarters of an inch to spare
once the boys had lowered the road.
It's known the king was barely five feet tall.
Astride a stallion, in an imposing frame,
and with fields of English oaks bowing down
for miles behind, which of us would have
cleared Ffestiniog Bridge unless the driver

had deflated all the tyres? The other
Van Dycks plus nineteen Rembrandts
and the Crown Jewels came by train as far as Bangor,
then disguised in vans delivering chocolate
to a disused mine. They stayed on display
for four years, a hidden exhibition whose lights
blazed all day, all night throughout
the Blackout

while in the quarry next door
men with torches cut pages of slate
into Empresses, Broad Countesses, Wide Ladies
and Duchesses Bach like some family
of royal women who roofed the world, by size.

SAMANTHA WYNNE-RHYDDERCH

STAFF ONLY
MSI

Writing Slate

Once, in earth's steady press, my tiny city's five factories
fed slate to a world's lust for letters. So I scratch this
with such dedication, draft by cleaning wounds with spit.
I sit, in my ergonomic chair, file open, and wait, blank
as a wet screen. Millennia. Heavy time til these hey presto
splitable lines of sediment tipped onto a spit clean screen.
This lace pattern of letters promises, but then curves,
gives for a place of weight which tugs toward the heart
of something. A vortex? A star. A small city, blackened
by inescape, reeling this thing back to its tightening core,
its town clock, and the longtime highstreet gathered and
smothered under all that cloud. With the press of a thumb
heavy weather smudges what the hell I meant to stone
quietness as I press backspace. Delete. To dead slate again

ALYS CONRAN

* RE-OPENING SOON -
UNDER NEW
MANAGMENT. *

III

NORTH COAST SWING

There could be temples

Llandudno Pier, August 2014

You run the gauntlet of *Amusement*
through a narrow souk of shouting stalls
– *Water Gun Gallery Just £3.50!*
No Photographs in Hats Until

You've Paid… and somewhere under the cliff face
of the Grand Hotel where
the scrolled rust of an iron staircase ends
like an accident, mid air –

somewhere there you cross the border
and, as if smoke cleared,
as if you were through the back of the wardrobe,
you step from tarmac onto boards

and this seems open water, sudden calm.

The long perspective of the boardwalk points to sea.
Buttressed with chinoiserie pavilions
it fixes stillness in a symmetry

that lets you sense,
beneath the slats beneath your feet,
mute music of the green sea working.

Souk runners stroll now, quietly,
breathing at ease as if a struggle's over,
dissipated in its own success.

The man in shorts, the woman in gold sandals
stand frozen at the rail
under the rock wave frozen in the Orme

and even the nippers can't break the spell
pelting towards that last pagoda
up the timber arrowshaft that's aimed

so purposeful, stock still, beyond the water.
And who are you, after all, to find this wanting,
that under the final cupola's pale spelter

instead of a Buddha stands a bright kiosk
holding out the offering of *Change*
or that against each angled wall

as in a chapter house the obelisks
of one-armed bandits blink, and have no arms at all,
and wait unchanging for your ghost oblation?

CHRISTOPHER MEREDITH

Rhyl Dawn

The promenade lights
go out, one by one,
leave vacancies for the sun.

*

A bulldog tugs a Bath chair
past abandoned waltzers.
Shops up-anchor.

*

Miss Sunny Rhyl's ghost
wears a yellow sash
over her grey macintosh.

*

Can you hear the waves?
Hush now. Are we too early
or too late, my love?

*

White seagull, black sky.
Black seagull, white sky.
The first spyglass opens its eye.

*

A crab's empty wallet
on the shore.
The first arcade opens its claw.

CHAN E

Varnishing Day

Today is for putting the finishing touches
to your work of art, for sealing in

the characters. A walk in the park,
which is what you can't do unescorted

in 1902. Setting up an easel in a public place
is out. As is roaming the cobbled streets

at dusk. How can you represent battles
or the crowning of Spanish kings without

attending a class where students draw
from life? You're stuck with subjects that don't move

or take their clothes off: a bowl of apples,
the view from a window, specimens

of rocks. You may work from reliefs and prints,
casts and Old Masters but if it breathes

don't go there. You might attempt a self-portrait
with bare arms or the back of a male nude

seated at a clavichord in a mirror
off left, but that's when it starts to show

you haven't had the training, that you have reached
vanishing point: the intersection of projections

of a set of perpendicular parallels onto
the picture plane, which is where some painters

disappear. All women. Watch them vanish
as you try and count them in on Varnishing Day.

Fly by

Vivian Hewitt flew past Rhyl in 1912, on his way to becoming the first man to fly from Wales to Ireland.

He rose, he rose above the glory
glory days, propellers in a tiz
around their cyclops eye,
new-fangled arms outstretched.
A boy-like bird, like make-believe
swooped above the upturned crowd
which simmered Sunday style
along the reels of silver,
silver promenade.

He cheered. They cheered
and watched this small high zoom
tightrope triumphant ways
across the cobbled sky
to trace a crown around
the penny a go, spend a penny,
penny farthing, penny world,
where fun-sized bathing bells parade
to the toot of colliseum bands
in the as yet untapped air.

He cheers. They cheer.
Even the domed pavilion doffs
its cap, and the parasols lift
their frilly lids. Even this fledgling girl,
tiny and fluorescent pink, who speeds
electric on her scooter beside
the still sepia sea, stops to lift
her momentary face, until
her penny eyes brim up
with all this cross-hatched sky.

Flat

You enter by the same door, stand on pause in the emptied stairwell, listen to the swill of holidays (in the webs of your fingers, backs of your knees, between your brows, those kind of plugholes) as they sink to the creases with old chewing gum, and flotsam jetsam bottle tops, dreams. You wait for the concierge to tip his bright cap, take your bad memory jacket, click his fingers for the boy to carry what you carry for a while – plastic bags, frozen peas, chicken drumsticks on special. Want. To your second floor place, half one of the best rooms in this establishment where ladies and gentlemen of class can take the sea air. Perhaps there was a lift, that kind of wood panelling, a porter to wind it up to your door so your feet, weary from drift and dutch beer, don't even touch as the staircase arpeggios its uncarpeted way under your trainers to the grand piano that stood open in your kitchenette. Play it again, your quiet fingers half an inch above its keys, rest in the up in the air before the unwind in discords and bad scales onto the bed, static of slot machine wins and falls, fall, sleepless. And all this applause.

ALYS CONRAN

Treading the Boards

How far can you go
to meet the sea
on its own terms,

walking over water
on a pier that strides
out on prosthetic

legs? You are heading away
from the mainland,
without once

getting your feet
wet, on some ocean-going
liner, yet never

seasick, disguised among
troupes of rollerskaters
and pierrots in parka hoods,

hiding in the tide
of day trippers who engulf
octagonal kiosks,

drawn towards a theatre
where you
are free to flirt,

balanced on boards
that taper away
into the rusting sun.

SAMANTHA WYNNE-RHYDDERCH

North Coast Swing

I

It's mild, no wind, and late sun rubs a pearl
through pastel cloud above the war memorial.
Between the shallow crescent of well-kept hotels
- Riverdale, Saint Kilda's, Brig-y-Don -
and the artificial shingle shore
they dumped to keep the sea at bay,
its back towards the waves, the swing band all in black

unclips its cases, tests the valves, unpacks
the girderwork of seats and music stands.
The seafront benches fill, the deckchairs gape
and the leader – white tie, black shirt, sleeked hair
ashy as the gentle sea – begins to time.
After the dead slow patter he turns
to face the band, the tide, and, routinely,

wags the stick. Count Basie it was, apparently,
who sang The Body Electric.
Mobility scooters, batteries whirring,
slow down to watch, and could make of it
a two tone joke that's off the beat, but
in fact they're pretty good, the shy band
etched against the sea. The dolorous

trumpet's muted as the colours
and it's nice that way. The crowd, mute too,
is palely curious. We don't know what to feel
except to feel that we don't know,
or know maybe that though this isn't an event
it's willing to be more than another act
of waiting in the place called Holiday.

2

Anyway, these timorous-smooth renditions
half ease us some where, some time other,
rubbing a cuff on a misted pane
till we can see, a little blurred,
how the leader's cormorant shape
's picked out elemental and absurd on cloud
or how that Trajan's column of ads

descanting on memorial
stands like a sample core drilled out of time,
the limp not limpid record of an age
as dreamed by Denmark Street and Radio Fun.
So, Jurassic-deep a withered poster calls
Remember The Times! A Good Ol'
1940s Knees Up! (Cast Of Eight)

and in a newer layer, Jimmy Osmond,
late career, huge-headed in a titch cartoon,
steps into Mickey Rooney's panto shoes,
then some am-drams doing bits from Brigadoon,
and closest to today's the seventies Motown Tribute
with Venue Cymru's guest band, The Detroits.
Let's hear it for those myth-frail cities burning gas!

For the abandoned too? For Kilda, say, Cwmorthin?
Somewhere eastward out of earshot the roads
are roaring still. Behind our backs unseen
the fractured centuries of this country press
in the raindrenched mass of farms and rock.
And we are not quite idling here, in neutral
tones, at the edge of something, mumbling song.

3

Not long now. The Body Electric,
via Pennsylvania, leads to a String of Pearls
that slip by the ear, translucent, cool
as the conductor's tie. He eyes his watch
then warily eyes us and turns away
for One More Time to lead the wave, to lead the tide,
to lead the pearly sky. Beyond

the blank mechanics of the band he sees
the nuances of grey stretch out immense, unhuman
into the toppled corridor of air
that rifts the sea and cloud.
Pale jazzhands of the windfarms drift
milling small change from the fitful breeze
as if a hundred clocks were running down

and almost at the weld of sky and sea
an oilrig, never quite in time,
snaps out a neon flag of yellow flame.
And done. In the dead air pause,
his baton down, before the soft rain of applause
he hears the water sigh against the rock
the shingle shift.

CHRISTOPHER MEREDITH

GRAND
HOTEL

IV

UNDER NEW MANAGEMENT

Between the Past and the Future

My images of North Wales are those of an outsider. They don't claim to 'capture' the place, or even describe it. Instead they may be seen as small poems, aiming to capture a mood or an atmosphere. North Wales is a strange and beautiful land, but I find myself confounded in trying to describe what it is today. It feels like a place that once had a strong identity – an identity now diminished along with the slate and farming industries.

What I see today is a place in transition. But transiting to where, I wonder? Wales has one foot firmly in the past, while the other foot hovers in mid-air, unsure where to land.

There are conundrums and juxtapositions everywhere. Nowhere is this more apparent than in Blaenau Ffestiniog. Here the slate mine is open for business. But instead of producing slate, it offers tourists the 'experience' of slate mining, by riding a tiny train that clatters through the dank and claustrophobic tunnels once used by working men, many of whom died of silicosis.

Sons of miners work here now as guides, dressed in vintage bowler hats and overalls, while overhead zip-wires hum as shrieking visitors glide overhead, having paid £50 for the thrill of flying between discarded slate mountains.

The town post office and bakery look unchanged, like fading snapshots from the 1950's. But down the road an internet café offers cappuccinos and free wi-fi.

There is a newly paved square with an old iron locomotive engine, salvaged and now brightly repainted like a child's toy. A former miner sits on a bench in the autumn sunshine. He seems lost in thought, but perhaps he's just thinking about where to have lunch … the bakery or the wi-fi café? The past or the future. Neither feels quite right … neither feels like the present.

ZED NELSON

Menu
UNRULY
CHILDREN
WILL BE TOLD
TO LEAVE

Argos

take out cash
Alliance Leicester
BARCLAYS
Lloyds TSB
Moving Home?
Use our Mail Redirection Service
NATIONAL SAVINGS
Post Office
OPEN
GIRO
Girobank
Stained notes like these are probably stolen
Need Help or Advice?
TOP PRIZE OF £8,000
BURIED TREASURE
MAXIMA
LITTLEWOODS
MOSS GUN!
COUNTY

CONWY

Photographs

Biographies

ALYS CONRAN's poetry, fiction and translations are to be found in several anthologies and magazines, most recently in *Stand* and *The Manchester Review*. Having studied and lived in Edinburgh, Barcelona and Manchester, she now has a scholarship to complete a doctorate in Creative Writing at home in Bangor. She lives in Bethesda with her husband, sculptor Joe Roberts, and writes from a shed that looks out over the Penrhyn Quarry.

MENNA ELFYN has published thirteen collections of poetry, also children's novels, libretti and plays for television and radio. Her most recent collection is *Merch Perygl (Danger's Daughter)*. Her bilingual volume, *Murmur,* appeared from Bloodaxe in 2012. A former Children's Poet Laureate for Wales, her work has been translated into eighteen languages. Currently Professor of Poetry and Director of Creative Writing at University of Wales Trinity Saint David, she was elected President of *PEN Wales* in 2015. www.mennaelfyn.co.uk

PAUL HENRY is the author of six collections of verse, the most recent of which is *Boy Running.* His selected poems, *The Brittle Sea,* has been reprinted by Seren in the UK and by Dronequill in India. Born in Aberystwyth, Paul came to poetry through songwriting and has presented arts programmes for BBC Radio Wales, Radio 3 and Radio 4.
www.paulhenrywales.co.uk

CHRISTOPHER MEREDITH is a novelist, poet and translator. He was born in Tredegar and lives in Brecon. In 2014 his first novel, *Shifts*, was shortlisted for the title of 'Greatest Welsh Novel of All Time'. His most recent novel is *The Book of Idiots*. His most recent collection of poems is *Air Histories*.
www.christophermeredith.webs.com

ZED NELSON has gained international recognition and numerous awards as a documentary photographer, with work that explores contemporary social issues. He has published three monograph photography books: *Gun Nation (2000), Love Me (2010)* and '*A Portrait of Hackney*' (2014). Exhibited at Tate Britain and the National Portrait Gallery, Nelson's work is also in the permanent collection of the Victoria & Albert Museum. Zed Nelson was born in Uganda and grew up in London, graduating from the University of Westminster.
www.zednelson.com

OWEN SHEERS is a poet, playwright and author. He has twice won Wales Book of the Year, in 2005 with his Zimbabwean non-fiction narrative *The Dust Diaries* and in 2014 with his verse drama *Pink Mist.* His play *The Two Worlds of Charlie F.* won the Amnesty International Freedom of Expression Award. His most recent novel is *I Saw A Man*. He lives with his wife and daughter in Talgarth. www.owensheers.co.uk

SAMANTHA WYNNE-RHYDDERCH's Picador collections were both shortlisted for Wales Book of the Year. In 2014 her pamphlet *Lime & Winter* was published by Rack Press and shortlisted for the Michael Marks Award. Samantha runs a writers' retreat on the Wales coastal path at www.writebythecoast.co.uk

Acknowledgements

The work produced here could not have been completed without the knowledge and guidance of the following individuals. The contributors are grateful for their kind help and time:
Catrin Roberts, Rhian Williams, Dafydd Jones, Dei 'Bo, John Blunden.

The Lledr Valley bridge featured in the photograph on page 13 was commissioned by the Camden Trust. It was designed and built by Jim Partridge and Liz Walmsley.

THE SLATE SEA

Published in 2015 by
The Camden Trust
43 Camden Passage, London, N1 8AE

ISBN: 978-0-9932509-0-3
A CIP record for this title is available from the British Library.

Designed and typeset by Isambard Thomas
www.isambardthomas.com

Printed and bound by Gomer Press,
Llandysul, Wales.

All proceeds from 'The Slate Sea'
will be used to support Camden Trust projects
with young persons.